REMEMBERING BOBBY ORR

B. ORR

REMEMBERING BOBBY ORR

A Celebration

CRAIG MacINNIS, EDITOR

A PETER GODDARD BOOK

Published in 1999 by Stoddart Publishing Co. Limited
34 Lesmill Road, Toronto, Canada M3B 2T6
180 Varick Street, 9th Floor, New York, New York 10014

Distributed in Canada by:
General Distribution Services Ltd.
325 Humber College Blvd., Toronto, Ontario M9W 7C3
Tel. (416) 213-1919   Fax (416) 213-1917
Email customer.service@ccmailgw.genpub.com

Distributed in the United States by:
General Distribution Services Inc.
85 River Rock Drive, Suite 202, Buffalo, New York 14207
Toll-free Tel. 1-800-805-1083   Toll-free Fax 1-800-481-6207
Email gdsinc@genpub.com

03   02   01   00   99   1   2   3   4   5

Canadian Cataloguing in Publication Data

Main entry under title: Remembering Bobby Orr

ISBN 0-7737-3196-2

1. Orr, Bobby, 1947–   . 2. Hockey Players – Canada – Biography. I. MacInnis, Craig

GV848.5.O7R45 1999   796.962'092   C99-931458-0

ART DIRECTION AND DESIGN: BILL DOUGLAS @ THE BANG

Page 114 constitutes a continuation of the copyright page.

We acknowledge for their financial support of our publishing program the Canada Council, the Ontario Arts Council, and the Government of Canada through the Book Publishing Industry Development Program (BPIDP).

Printed and bound in Canada

Contents

HOCKEY'S ALL-TIME GREATEST: MAKING THE CASE FOR BOBBY ORR   01
by Craig MacInnis

FIVE-STAR GENERAL: BOBBY ORR — FUTURE SUPERSTAR?   13
by Paul Rimstead, January 11, 1964

WATCHING BOBBY: A CHILD'S-EYE VIEW OF THE YOUNG SUPERSTAR   17
by Craig MacInnis

PORTRAIT OF THE ARTIST AS A YOUNG BACHELOR: A FEMALE   29
PERSPECTIVE ON THE ORR PHENOMENON
by Rosie DiManno

FROM ZEROES TO HEROES: THE MAKING OF THE BIG BAD BRUINS   45
by Craig MacInnis

SNAPSHOT OF THE CENTURY   64
by Craig MacInnis

MEMORIES OF BEANTOWN: REMEMBERING BOBBY'S LEGACY   69
by Jonathan Kahn

RATING ORR: HOW GREAT WAS HE?   77
by Frank Orr

CHERRY ON ORR: AN INTERVIEW WITH DON CHERRY   93
by Craig MacInnis

WHAT THEY SAID: QUOTABLE QUOTES ON BOBBY ORR   109

CAREER STATISTICS   112

CAREER HIGHLIGHTS   113

HOCKEY'S ALL-TIME
GREATEST

MAKING THE CASE FOR BOBBY ORR

With the new millennium upon us, there is an urge — maybe even a deep-seated need — to sort through hockey's cluttered mythology and extract its essence. Put a name to the game. If baseball was Babe Ruth and basketball was Michael Jordan and football was Joe Montana (or Johnny Unitas, or John Elway, or Jim Brown — take your pick), who then was hockey?

Wayne Gretzky? His retirement last spring seemed an apt end-of-century gesture: The exit of #99 in '99. For many, Gretzky's departure was the century's perfect coda, the send-off of an individual who not only dominated hockey for nearly two decades but whose media-friendly image forged new pathways for the NHL's migration to the southern States. Leaving as he did before the calendar turned over to 2000, all but ensures Gretzky's status as player of the century. Certainly his list of career achievements, including 92 goals in a single season, makes a compelling case.

But just as Academy Award-contending films that are released in December tend to fare better than those from earlier in the year, hockey's older heroes have been overlooked in the headlong rush to canonize the game's Hundred-Year Man. Nominees for this distinction include Gordie Howe, Mario Lemieux, Guy Lafleur,

Rocket Richard, Eddie Shore, Doug Harvey, and countless others. But we are not here to discuss the worthy runners-up. We are here to give our vote to Bobby Orr. Hands down. No contest.

When one thinks of the shape of the modern-era game and the role of its most brilliant offensive-minded defencemen, from Gretzky's great Oilers teammate Paul Coffey to Dallas Stars' point man Sergei Zubov, from Detroit veteran Larry Murphy to young Toronto Maple Leaf Bryan Berard, it is impossible to imagine any of them being what they are today without Orr's pioneering influence.

THOUGH HE PLAYED JUST NINE FULL SEASONS IN THE NHL, ORR LEFT NOT ONLY A LEGACY OF STATISTICAL EXCELLENCE BUT A BLUEPRINT FOR THE GAME'S FUTURE DEFENCEMEN: TWO-WAY MOBILITY, FREE-WHEELING PUCK MOVEMENT, AND END-TO-END (OR SIDE-TO-SIDE) RUSHES.

Glen Sather, an astute hockey teacher and a teammate of Orr's in Boston, took that very formula with him to Edmonton, where his Oilers dominated the NHL for the better part of a decade.

"There was no one ever like him. Not even close," says Orr's Bruins coach Don Cherry, who takes time out from his "Coach's Corner" duties on *Hockey Night in Canada* to share his memories as Bobby's bench boss later in this book.

The fact that many teams in this era of reckless expansion have forsaken Orr's lessons in favour of the "clutch and grab" and the "neutral-zone trap" only makes his contributions more poignant – and resonant.

Orr spoiled us, those of us who were lucky enough to see him in his prime, those of us, who in our own youth and innocence, assumed hockey would always be played the way he played it.

He was just an 18-year-old fresh off the Oshawa Generals junior team when he joined the Boston Bruins for the 1966-67 season. That year, he not only won the Calder Trophy, the league's rookie-of-the-year award, but he was also named to the Second All-Star Team, despite the onset of knee injuries that would plague him till the end.

OVER THE NEXT EIGHT SEASONS, THE NORRIS TROPHY, FOR BEST DEFENCEMAN, NEVER LEFT HIS MANTLEPIECE.

He was the first rearguard to win the NHL scoring title, a staggering feat which he managed twice, in 1969-70 and 1974-75.

To understand just how dominant Orr was at the peak of his career – and how he revolutionized the role of the defenceman – simply look at the scoring stats for the 1969-70 campaign. Orr finished first overall with 120 points. Teammate and perennial offensive threat Phil Esposito finished with 99 points, 21 fewer than Orr. Stan Mikita, in third place, had 86 points. The defenceman nearest him that year was Carol Vadnais, a nifty backliner who notched a relatively paltry 44 points, followed by Pat Stapleton with 42.

More important, Orr's impact was team-wide. His rebuilt Bruins captured two Stanley Cups (in 1970 against St. Louis and 1972 against New York),

Orr fights off the Leafs' Pete Stemkowski for the puck.

rescuing Boston and its long-suffering fans from the doldrums of mediocrity (they hadn't won a Cup since 1940-41).

Orr's legend, unlike Gretzky's, or that graybeard of longevity, Gordie Howe's, seems somehow more complete for its brevity. Every time a game was on the line, Orr was there, making the most of each opportunity.

IN BOTH OF THE BRUINS' CHAMPIONSHIP SEASONS HE SCORED THE STANLEY CUP–WINNING GOAL.

"You want to know what turned this game around?" asked Rangers' captain Vic Hadfield after his Blueshirts lost to the Bruins in six games. "It was the same thing that turned the whole series around — Bobby Orr."

By 1976, an injury-hobbled Orr turned free agent and signed with Chicago, where his career was to end with a whimper. That same autumn, however, he skated for Team Canada in the inaugural Canada Cup, leading the Canadians past the Czechs and claiming the tournament's MVP award.

Don Cherry has noted that this was "the last thing" most fans remember of Orr's career, his knees already battered beyond repair but his heart and brain still striving to conjure a win in the battle for world bragging rights.

Orr in his familiar up-ice position, moves in on the Leafs' Bernie Parent.

This is not a book about Orr's life after hockey. Nor is it an investigation into Orr's relationship with Alan Eagleson, the disgraced agent and former hockey czar. Those stories have already been told, probably once too often.

Any retrospective of Orr's career, already well documented by the statisticians and puck pundits, needs the prism of personal experience, a human filter through which we might recover an emotional sense of what he meant to the people who watched him play.

Remembering Bobby Orr offers warm first-person recollections of what Orr meant to those whose lives he touched, larded with famous and rare photographs that capture the Parry Sound native in action and in repose.

Jonathan Kahn, who spent the late 1970s at university in Boston, recalls how Orr permanently changed the Massachusetts sports landscape, and how Kahn's college dorm Kevin neighbour developed a fanatical obsession for "Num-bah fo-ah."

Frank Orr, the Hockey Hall of Fame sportswriter, chats with some of the greats of the game, including Harry Sinden and Gerry Cheevers, to etch a fresh portrait of the NHL's greatest defenceman.

Don Cherry offers his up-close impressions of Orr, including two of the greatest goals Orr ever scored, and sportswriter Rosie DiManno, who admits to a "girlhood crush" on Bruins' goalie Cheevers, explores the masculine mystique of the Orr-era Bruins, noting that the freckled, straight-laced rookie was humorously at odds with the emerging counterculture of the late 1960s.

As someone who cut his hockey teeth in that era, I also have a personal link with the game's greatest player. When I was nine, I watched Orr's Oshawa Generals win a bitterly fought, seven-game playoff series against my hometown heroes, the St. Catharines Black Hawks.

Looking back on it now, that seems the moment in my life when everything opened up in front of me, when all the possibilities of the world could be found in the searing athleticism of a jug-eared, crew-cut phenom from Northern Ontario.

I hope this book recaptures that same feeling for anyone who ever saw him play, and maybe even for some who didn't.

— Craig MacInnis

FIVE-STAR
GENERAL

BOBBY ORR — FUTURE SUPERSTAR?

by Paul Rimstead, Toronto Star, *January 11, 1964*

OSHAWA — If Bobby Orr ever proves to be only human, strong men in Boston will break down and weep.

What's so special about this 15-year-old youngster from Parry Sound? Nothing, really, if you see him in his street clothes. He's a grade 9 student at Oshawa's R.S. McLaughlin vocational school, has a blond crewcut, and spends the summers back home, working in uncle Howard's butcher shop.

The transformation takes place when Bobby slips into his Oshawa Generals' uniform. Boston Bruins, who haven't much to crow about, call him the greatest hockey prospect in the country.

They get few arguments.

It's hard to compare this young defenceman to another player because no one can recall anyone as prominent at such a tender age.

For instance — last season, while a grade 8 pupil at Parry Sound, Orr commuted to Oshawa and made the second all-star team in the Metro Junior A League. He was only 14 and jumped from bantam to Junior A hockey. This season, in the tougher OHA Provincial League, Bobby has scored 19 goals and has 23 assists — as a defenceman. He has 22 games in which to break the record of 25 goals set last year by defenceman Jacques Laperriere of Montreal Canadiens.

The young warrior, freckles and all.

OSHAWA GENERALS 1963-64

Back row, left to right: Bobby Orr, Mike Dubeau, Bill Smith, Bob Kilgour, Chris Roberts, Terry Lane and Darryl Leach.

Centre row, left to right: George Vail, Rod Zane, Bill Little, Bill Lastic, Ron Buchanan, Danny O'Shea (Capt.), Jim Blair, Rick Gay, Brian Fletcher, Wayne Cashman and Nick Beverley.

Front row, left to right: Joe Childerhose, Ian Young, Jim Cherry (Coach), Stan Waylett (Trainer), Wren Blair (General Manager), Dennis Gibson and Gerry Blair (Asst. General Manager).

"HE PLAYS 35–40 MINUTES A GAME AND HE'S THE TEAM LEADER. **HE CAN'T MISS. HE'D MAKE THE NHL AT ANY POSITION."**

And he has five years of junior hockey left!

Boston's only concern is that you can never tell for sure when a player is only 15. He looks like the superstar Boston has been seeking for years – but they remember Dallas Smith.

Smith was called up to the National Hockey League when only 18. Now he's in the minors. The only possible flaw in Orr is his size – 5-foot-9-inches and 160 pounds. However, Bruins are quick to point out that last year he weighed only 135 and stood 5-6.

Four NHL clubs – Toronto, Detroit, Montreal, and Boston – were after Orr and he picked Bruins because, "they're a team of the future. They're rebuilding and I want to be part of that building program," says Bobby.

Doug Orr, his father, played intermediate hockey with the Parry Sound Shamrocks. Together, they listened to the various pitches. "They're all good talkers," smiles Bobby.

Wren Blair, the first to talk to him, scored for Boston. "He's a combination of Doug Harvey and Eddie Shore," enthuses Blair.

"Reminds me of Red Kelly when Red was in his last year at St. Mikes," says coach Jim Cherry. "He plays 35-40 minutes a game and he's the team leader. He can't miss. He'd make the NHL at any position."

Orr (top, far left) with the 1963-64 Oshawa Generals.

WATCHING
BOBBY

A CHILD'S-EYE VIEW OF THE YOUNG SUPERSTAR

by Craig MacInnis

When I was nine, Bobby Orr broke my heart. Left it there in pieces, along with the popcorn boxes and rubber galoshes that littered the Oshawa Civic Auditorium ice at the end of game seven. In the annals of great hockey series, few historians ever mention the 1966 Junior A quarter-final between Orr's Oshawa Generals and the team I then rooted for with a kid's blind passion, the St. Catharines Black Hawks. But for me it was the Big One, a combative, seesaw fortnight when a 17-year-old kid from Parry Sound changed the face of hockey by taking the game, single-handedly, to a new plateau.

I have never seen or felt anything like it since – and, frankly, I don't know if I could handle it if it were to come along again. Without exaggerating, it was the moment that my life passed from innocence into experience, the moment when I dimly began to understand hockey not only as a game but as savage allegory.

Essayists and blue-line pundits have often probed the tribal ferocity of junior hockey, how a community's self-image finds expression in the fortunes of the local team and how such allegiances reveal something about ourselves that we do not always prefer to advertise. But advertise it we do, screaming at bad calls, cheering goals, booing at penalties, and generally transferring our fears and aspirations onto a group of high-school-age athletes.

Orr takes to the ice at the old Hamilton Forum.

This was exactly the case as Oshawa prepared to meet St. Catharines, a battle of southern Ontario's two General Motors' towns, a contest that would accord bragging rights to the winner. The loser? The loser would feel an emptiness deep in the pit of the stomach, and would nurse a hockey-induced ague through the long summer that stretched ahead.

It should have been a mismatch, pitting the blue-collar Black Hawks against the talent-rich Generals, whose roster, in addition to Orr, included the brilliant netminder Ian Young and such future NHLers as Danny O'Shea and Wayne Cashman.

Cashman, who would later earn distinction as a hard-nosed teammate of Orr in Boston, nearly sheared my skull off in game four when an altercation broke out between him and a fan seated directly behind me. The fan's name was Mr. Brown, who, like my father and I, was a season ticket holder to Hawks games. We sat in the front row, ice level reds, near the penalty box. Mr. Brown, who was usually friendly and full of good-natured jibes ("Hey ref, you dropped your white cane!") sat behind us in Row B with his wife. Mr. Brown had a famous temper, though, when things weren't going well for St. Catharines (which was often), and on this occasion he taunted Cashman until he took the bait.

Waving his stick menacingly, Cashman grazed my forehead with his blade as he tried to lay a tattooing on Mr. Brown. It is one thing to admire the power and animal force of hockey from the safety of one's rail seat. It is something again to have that power surge over the boards (there was no protective glass at Garden City Arena in those days) and confront you with its cold breath.

Hockey, so liquid and mesmerizing on ice, turns solid and deranged when

Oshawa's top-ranking General.

its force escapes into the stands, like freeing an Evil Genie from a bottle. I was scared witless. Until quite recently, it didn't even seem real. More like a dream I'd had, although my father remembers it well enough. The incident even made the local newspaper, as this account from the *St. Catharines Standard* of March 14, 1966, attests: "On the last play of the first period, a St. Catharines fan grabbed Wayne Cashman's stick, Cashman finally pulled it free, then swung at the spectator, breaking the stick over the boards. [The referee] and the two linesmen missed the entire incident but the fan was removed, apparently for his own protection."

Speaking from a nine-year-old partisan's standpoint, it was easy to hate the Generals after that. Especially Orr, whose mastery of the game was so thorough that he seemed to toy with the opposition. It's not that he was smart-alecky like certain other junior stars of the era, such as his future Bruin teammate Derek Sanderson, a member of the Niagara Falls Flyers in the mid-'60s and a junior adversary of Orr. Sanderson favored a constant smirk and a laughing gaze that revealed his contempt for the other team. Orr never seemed cocky or contemptful, even when he was hammering someone into the boards.

WITH HIS FRECKLES AND BRUSH CUT, HE WAS MORE LIKE DENNIS THE MENACE RECAST AS A GEOMETRY BUFF.

He had a trick in those days that showed how hockey, for him, was a series of Pythagorean theorems.

Waiting in his own end with the puck and positioning himself two or three feet in front of the end boards, he would invite an opponent to forecheck him into oblivion. Just as the onrushing checker would bear down on him, Orr would

21

backhand the puck against the end boards, dip to his left, and follow his bank shot up ice past the bewildered checker, who was, by then, ten feet behind the play.

In that same game in which Cashman went berserk, Orr scored two goals in a losing Oshawa effort, but more importantly, he asserted his dominance with savvy and toughness that would eventually wear down the entire Black Hawks roster.

No one, I think, would want to describe Orr, now or then, as a dirty player. However, his grit easily matched his agility, a fact lost on those who only recall his brilliant end-to-end rushes and scoring feats. In the 1965–66 regular season, Orr, playing defence, finished third in Ontario Hockey Association scoring with 94 points, behind only Peterborough Petes forwards Andre Lacroix, with 120 points, and Danny Grant, with 96.

To give you an idea of his offensive prowess, Orr placed ahead of Montreal Jr. Canadiens' star forward Jacques Lemaire (93 points), who had the hardest shot in the league. Orr also bested such future NHL stars as Mickey Redmond (92 points) and Sanderson (76).

Most people watched Orr for his offensive smarts, but Orr played hard – even mean – at both ends of the rink. Consider the check that he laid on Hawks forward Ken Laidlaw in the dying minutes of game four, reported in the *St. Catharines Standard*: "Orr grabbed Laidlaw by the scruff of the neck, shook him like a limp rag, then kicked the skates out from under him."

And when Orr wasn't making checks or scoring goals, he was blocking them, sliding into the crease to cover for Ian Young after Oshawa had pulled its goalie for an extra attacker. Once during the series, the Hawks actually managed to score on Orr the Goalie: "Orr scurried back to guard the net but [Hawks forward Steve] Latinovich . . . swung a one-hand bounce shot over Orr's stick."

In the dressing room after the game, Hawks' manager Ken Campbell cracked, "At least we've found that Orr has a weakness. He's not too good in goal." Maybe not, but everywhere else the toll was mounting on a beleaguered Black Hawks squad. By the time game seven rolled around, it seemed as if half the St. Catharines lineup was on the limp, all due to Orr.

Standard sports editor Jack Gatecliff itemized the damage: "Willie Terry watched the final game on crutches after suffering a badly bruised ankle Friday night while stopping a drive from Orr.

"Paul Terbenche, perhaps the best blocking defenceman in junior hockey, was unable to continue after the 13-minute mark in the first period Saturday afternoon. The native of Port Hope had a fingernail torn off with one of Orr's shots, then stopped another with his forearm."

It was as if Orr's greatness couldn't help but have corrosive side effects, that anyone who drew too close, or tried to stop him, would wither in the heat of his genius.

* * *

The seventh and deciding game of the series was played in Oshawa on Saturday afternoon, March 19, 1966. My father and I had attended game six on Friday night in St. Catharines (a 4–3 win for the Hawks), and I managed to coax the old man into making the two hour drive to Oshawa to see the finale.

One can never say enough about a father willing to do that for his kid. I learned that day that hockey, in addition to everything else, was the common ground my father and I needed to reach across to each other.

Unfortunately, the game was over almost before we'd found our seats. The Hawks, having run out of energy and manpower, succumbed in a one-sided laugher, 8–1. Orr had three assists. I remember the embarrassment, when, in the third period and the score 7–0, a bored Oshawa fan seated in front of us shouted: "C'mon, St. Catharines, at least make it interesting."

This was what I feared most, looking bad in the enemy's den.

As if to rub it in, Orr, at the end of the game, was treated to a rousing version of "Happy Birthday" by the jubilant Oshawa boosters. The next day, Sunday, March 20, was his 18th birthday. During the little on-ice ceremony, Orr was also presented with a transistor radio and a cake.

He accepted the fans' accolades with typical humility: "All of these guys are a part of this," he said, pointing to his teammates. "They've been playing great."

The drive home that evening was one of the longest of my young life, but by the time we pulled into our driveway in St. Catharines I had weakly resolved to cheer the Generals on in their quest for the Memorial Cup. With the Hawks gone, it only seemed right to go with Orr. He had administered such a thrashing to the home side — and with such show-stopping verve — that the boundaries of municipal allegiance no longer seemed relevant.

Even nine-year-olds recognize greatness when they have the privilege to watch it up close. Especially when greatness rubs their noses in it.

Orr defends his net against a junior attack.

"HE'S THE SMARTEST PLAYER I'VE EVER SEEN," SAID MY DAD, AND HE HAD SEEN MOST OF THEM, FROM EDDIE SHORE TO DOUG HARVEY.

"He's the smartest player I've ever seen," said my dad, and he had seen most of them, from Eddie Shore to Doug Harvey.

In subsequent playoffs that spring, Orr's Generals beat Scotty Bowman's Montreal Jr. Canadiens, then took out the Kitchener Rangers in five games to win the OHA title. From there, it was on to a date in North Bay, Ontario, where they slaughtered the hopelessly overmatched Trappers in four straight games.

The *Oshawa Times* reported, "Orr, who scored eight goals and assisted on 14 others in the series, harried North Bay forwards with puck control when Oshawa was shorthanded. Once he skated the length of the ice and all the way back, chased by four North Bay players."

Led by Orr, the Generals would go on to defeat the Shawinigan Bruins of the Quebec league before losing in the Memorial Cup final to the Edmonton Oil Kings in six games. Orr suffered a pulled groin in that series and played only spottily, as if providing foreshadowing for the series of injuries that were to cut short his pro career.

In Oshawa, they still talk about losing that Cup — and what might've been. But none of that really mattered. Not to me. Not then. In the spring of 1966, not a mile from my house on Cliff Road, I saw the greatest hockey player of the twentieth century play in a little bandbox rink called Garden City Arena, watched him pass and shoot and slide to block shots, watched him rush past Black Hawks as if they were standing still.

When a life's moments are tallied up and final stock is taken, it's not a bad thing to be able to say, "I got to see Orr play when he was just a kid. I was even there for his 18th birthday party."

Orr and Orr: Bobby poses with brother Ron.

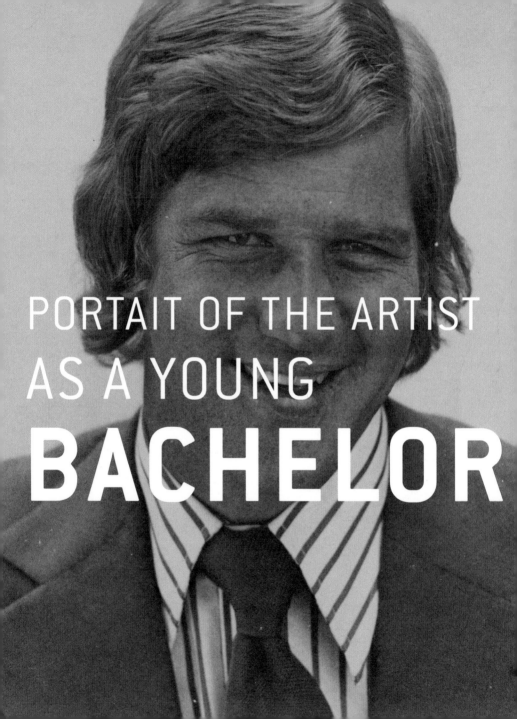

PORTAIT OF THE ARTIST
AS A YOUNG
BACHELOR

A FEMALE PERSPECTIVE ON THE ORR PHENOMENON

by Rosie DiManno

Bobby Orr was a geek. That crewcut that revealed every knob on his skull, that lumpy nose, the thick creases in a fleshy face and a too-small mouth for the broad plummet of his jaw. Over the years, Robert Gordon Orr has grown into his face, become the man in middle-age that more properly suits his countenance, even affords him a degree of elegance.

But in 1966, when the man-child first seized continental fame as a rookie with the Boston Bruins, Orr was this quasi-freakish creature who reinforced the unsexy reputation of professional hockey. He was no Joe Namath. He wasn't even Jim McKenny, former Toronto Maple Leaf defenceman and Toronto Marlboro grad who emerged from his junior hockey chrysalis at the same time, and who was promoted by Leafs coach Punch Imlach as the next-best thing to the greatest thing to come out of the pubescent ranks.

McKenny, now there was a cool dude. Ruggedly handsome, with a whiff of anti-establishment recklessness to his character. His hair was thick and shaggy, vaguely mophead mod. McKenny offered a rare glimpse of mid-'60s sass in a game that often seemed locked in to a '40s ethos. A girl could dream about doing naughty things to McKenny that went well beyond running her hands through that coif. To fantasize even the most clumsy of teenage intimacies with Orr was

. . . icky, like making out with your twerpy kid brother.

Orr was always other-worldly to the puck groupies and groupettes — the unpolished girls, I mean, not the more conniving ones who were prepared to go beyond the realm of imagination and shrieking adolescent crushes. Despite the endless media references to his tender years, this 18-year-old NHLer was the hockey equivalent of a brown noser, the brilliant but hopelessly uncool high school nerd who would likely grow up to discover a cure for acne but would never get a date to the prom.

Of course, Orr never went to the prom. He never went beyond Grade 11, not in the normal academic progression of his teenage peers. The kid attended a vocational school in Oshawa, for goodness sake, enrolled there to fit the hockey aspirations of a boy — the third of five children born to Doug and Alva Orr, she a coffee shop waitress, he a factory worker at Canadian Industries Ltd., an explosives firm — who left his Parry Sound family abode at 14 to play with the Oshawa Generals. Come the summer, he toiled in his uncle's butcher shop. I doubt whether he ever drank beer out back beyond the school yard, or snapped a girl's brassiere in the hallway, or fumbled awkwardly to buy prophylactics at the drug store. Orr with the circular indentation of a rubber in his wallet? Puh-leeze. He was the kind of young man every parent dreamed that a daughter would bring home — courteous, shy, deferential, and unmistakably trustworthy. All the qualities that would render him unspeakably unattractive to a teenage girl. I know, I was one.

"I'm scared skinny of this," Orr was actually quoted as saying, as he ventured into the realm of the NHL, a legion of sportswriters in tow. Scared skinny? And then, on one occasion when he was invited to make a public appearance:

"I'm no shucks as a speaker."

Well, no shuck-ing kidding. It was the '60s, on the cusp of the Age of Aquarius. Rebellion was percolating on college campuses, birth control pills had given females unprecedented sexual freedom, American students were starting to protest a conscripted war in the jungles of southeast Asia. The British invasion in music and art and fashion had hit U.S. shores. The heady aroma of marijuana was in the air. Hair got long and longer, bellbottoms got wide and wider. The world of youth divided into hippies and greasers. By 1968 — when you could just see the beginning of the Big Bad Bruins — the entire Western world convulsed in chaos: protesters and police clashing in the streets, violence at the Democratic convention in Chicago, free love on the hoof, and Art Linkletter's acid-addled daughter taking a header out the window.

ORR DIDN'T FIT INTO THIS WORLD. WHILE THE REST OF US WERE MUSING OVER WHETHER TO DROP GRADE 10 MATH, HE HAD A PERSONAL AGENT — FUTURE FELON ALAN EAGLESON — HELPING HIM DECIDE WHICH OF THE FOUR NHL TEAMS IN HOT PURSUIT — TORONTO, DETROIT, MONTREAL, AND BOT-TOM-DWELLING BOSTON — SHOULD RECEIVE HIS FAVOUR.

* * *

While we, the nascent Baby Boomers, sought privacy from our parents and dreamed of crash pads, Orr was back in Peabody, a serene middle-class suburb 19 miles north of the Boston Garden, sharing an apartment with three other guys

TO FANTASIZE EVEN THE MOST CLUMSY OF TEENAGE
INTIMACIES WITH ORR WAS . . . ICKY, LIKE MAKING OUT WITH
YOUR TWERPY KID BROTHER.

and wearing an apron around his waist as he washed the dishes. His precious domesticities were chronicled by an over-the-hill press that really believed Orr was the cat's pajamas. Some kinda hunk. A "teeny-whopper," as one scribe put it. Goodness, they tried hard, these hockey beat writers, to juice the sexy factor on Orr's behalf, to elevate him to the upper echelons of new-wave jocks who bristled with 'tude and self-entitlement, even as they, the chroniclers, continued to nod approvingly, in print, at Orr's oft-mentioned self-effacement.

Was there ever anything as silly as the repeated allusions to Orr's ostensibly hip bachelor lifestyle, and the sober inquiries about his relationship with girls, girls, girls? Wren Blair, then of the Bruins and later general manager of the Generals, is the fellow who sold the Orr family on the merits of Boston, where the kid phenom would step directly into a starting job on the blueline. But Blair, who had a great influence over the young man, was wise to the perils of professional sports. Orr had an abundance of fundamental skills, yet Blair cautioned that the teen was a babe in the woods when it came to other, peripheral matters.

"Publicity, backslappers, and the cause of the biggest casualty list in hockey – girls," said Blair. "Girls bug hockey players. They hang around the dressing room after a game hoping for a pick-up. They'd like nothing better than to hook a guy – especially in junior hockey where these kids are as big with the teenage crowd as the Beatles." Well, maybe in Oshawa, and Flin Flon, and Medicine Hat. In Toronto, teenage girls would rather have thrown their panties at Mickey Dolenz (The Monkees!) than at John Lennon, much less Bobby Orr, even if he was hauling down at least $45,000, including bonuses, in his rookie season. In the hockey universe, only Bobby Hull, Gordie Howe, and Jean Beliveau were making more.

No one seemed more aware of the behavioural restrictions imposed on Orr

than Orr himself. "You see, this is what I've discovered about being sort of in the public eye," he told one correspondent. "You begin to realize there's a responsibility. You could do a lot of harm. You can't be anything less than a gentleman at all times because everybody is watching. And when people listen carefully to what you say, you have to think about it and say the right things."

Was there anything more contrary, from a teenager's perspective, to the temperament of those times? At training camp in London, Ontario, that September of 1966, Orr drew the grizzled Johnny Bucyk — known as "The Chief" before native Indian references were frowned upon in the sports lexicon — as his roommate. This was no casual coincidence. Better the boy should share a room with a mature veteran like Bucyk than be exposed to the more rowdy inclinations of his 20-something teammates. Orr went around calling his bunkmate "Mr. Bucyk" until he was, shall we say, dissuaded.

Orr captured the Calder Trophy, of course, as best rookie, at the end of that debut season. He also hurt his knee in a collision with teammate Bob Leiter during a charity game that summer and was placed in a cast. But only the jittery old coots in the Bruins executive suite were overly concerned. Mostly they were furious that permission for the exhibition appearance had not been obtained from the mother club.

Inset: *Orr and teammate Gilles Marotte.*
Opposite: *Orr wards off the Habs'*
Henri Richard.

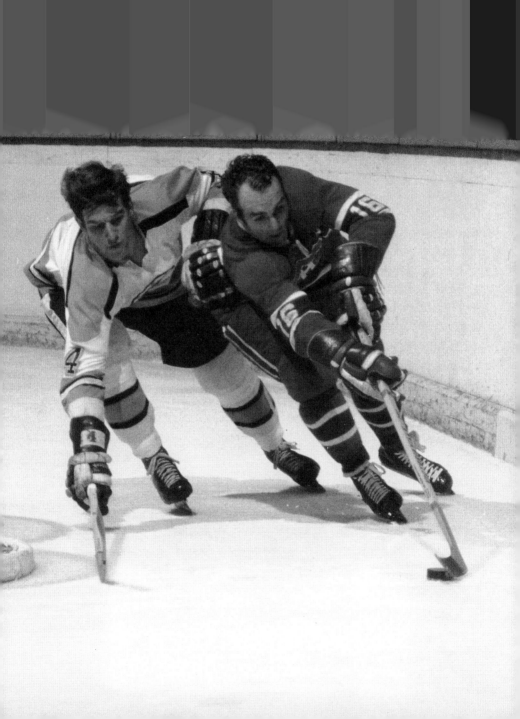

It was the beginning of the end, as we now know, even before Orr had begun his sophomore season. There would be more collisions, more injuries to both knees, more operations, more cartilage removed until there was nothing left holding the joints together and Orr was hobbled. But that unfair end was still several years down the road.

At the time, Orr couldn't even legally order a drink in a bar, and Lord knows he would probably never break the libation laws. A visiting writer did spot a box of beer empties at the Orr residence in Peabody one autumn eve. In his defence, Orr could have pointed an accusing finger at any of his three roommates: veteran goalkeeper Eddie Johnston, sophomore defenceman Gary Doak, and assistant trainer John Forristall. So much for an unexamined private life.

That three-bedroom pad was owned by Dick Williams, then-manager of the Boston Red Sox, whose wife had phoned Orr and offered the winter sublet. While Doak and Johnston would eventually move out, Forristall lingered as Orr's chaperone until the future Mrs. Orr appeared — but more about that later. In 1970, Forristall spun tales of Orr the Homemaker for newspaper writer Trent Frayne: "When the broads come to the house, they're speechless. The place is spotless. Even the guys on the team are surprised when they come over for a party. They think we had a cleaning lady in because it was a special occasion. But it's always like that. If Bobby passes an ashtray and it's dirty, he cleans it. I do the same. I cook — roast beef, chicken, things like that — and he does the dishes."

At this stage of Orr's career — one Stanley Cup, another on the horizon — some Boston scribes were even suggesting that he was more popular than former Red Sox star Ted Williams had ever been in Beantown. By then, Orr had adopted a few of the high-livin' accouterments: a big shining Cadillac Eldorado, suits

from Lou Myles in Toronto, a rented two-garage Cape Cod bungalow in subur-
ban Lynnfield (with Forristall), where many Bruins still live with their families to
this day. But Orr continued talking the modest superstar game.

"People think athletes lead a pretty fast life," he said. "They think they drink
a lot and spend all their time at parties or in bars. I don't come into town much
to go to the clubs. There's always some drunk who wants to prove he's tough by
fighting with you or something."

He was then receiving some 300 fan letters a week. And for the life of me,
I still can't believe that many of them were from pining females, although Orr did
once hand around a missive from a stewardess who insisted that she'd been
promised a date, and here was her phone number in case he'd lost it. But more
of the mail came from little boy fans and pre-teen girls, like the gaggle who
signed their names to a 50-foot long letter. She-fans who didn't know the first
thing about seduction.

Forristall claimed they had to keep changing their home phone number
because women found it out all the time and called and called and called. True,
by 1970 Orr had started to let his hair down a bit, no doubt by the influence of
some hipper, less-obedient Bruin teammates, most particularly the self-professed
stud, Derek Sanderson. The mustachioed bad boy from Niagara Falls got a photo
spread in *Maclean's*, a national Canadian magazine, that showed him reclining,
immodestly, with bathrobe partly open, on a circular bed. Sanderson was the
Elvis of NHL hockey, faux leopard-skin tastes and all. So Orr began wearing
stovepipe pants and partly unbuttoned silk shirts, his straw-coloured hair curled
over his collar. But, sorry, he still looked like a geek.

The Anything Goes '70s did not rest lightly on his shoulders. Reporters

41

Derek "Turk" Sanderson, branding the
Bruins with his long-haired swagger (top).
Even Orr let his hair down.

continued streaming to his house, now that Orr was "of age," and found him still doing the dishes. But at least there was some hint that the cog in the Bruins' engine was no longer leading a celibate life.

"We know lots of girls," he told one visitor, even as he described how he and "Frosty" liked to dust and mop "and change the bedding."

Was there anyone special? he was asked. "No, not really. I want to do too much. I want to go too many places. It wouldn't be fair to any girl to get married yet. Hockey is a job and you do it sensibly. Guys drink, and some smoke. Most of the players are married and the single guys like to go out with girls. But before a game you wouldn't drink, and the night before a game you wouldn't have a date. You have to train yourself because if your body is that much stronger, you play that much better."

In early 1971, Orr was preparing to step onto the ice at Maple Leaf Gardens for the third period of a game when an unidentified woman pushed out of the crowd and punched him in the face. "I don't know what got into that dumb broad," Orr said afterwards, in what would now be considered horribly incorrect language. "I was walking in front of Ted Green when all of a sudden this dame punches me in the face and jumps back into the crowd. She had a lousy punch. She needs a lot of work on the fast bag."

Less than a year after the incident with the Toronto woman, the *Toronto Star* reported breathlessly, "Bobby Orr Engaged to Florida Teacher." There was a picture of a young woman, a winsome damsel with blonde hair pulled back in a pony tail. She looked a little bit like Swinging London actress Julie Christie. Her name was Peggy Wood, a Detroit native and "former Red Wing fan" who was a speech therapist at the Exceptional Child Center in Fort Lauderdale. Orr had met her during a vacation and, on Christmas Day in 1972, he presented her with a 4-carat diamond engagement ring. There was no great sigh of regret from the female public.

The following September, when Orr was 25, the couple wed in a hush-hush ceremony performed by a Presbyterian minister in Parry Sound, just before the start of training camp. Orr spent the morning fishing. The bride wore a pale blue pant suit. The reception afterwards was a joint party, grafted onto a farewell gathering for Orr's brother, Ron, who was on his way to Binghamton, New York, to coach hockey. How romantic. Mr. and Mrs. Orr dropped by Alan Eagleson's home in Clarkson, just west of Toronto, before continuing on to their new two-bedroom apartment on the 15th floor of the Prudential Life building in downtown Boston. In due course, two baby boys were born. Then came charges of tax evasion, an Eagleson saga, and an ill-advised move to the Chicago Blackhawks. The great career had lasted only 12 seasons. His knees were a mess. But he finally had the face, and the wisdom, of a man. I think I could kinda go for Bobby now.

Rosie DiManno, a longtime Boston rooter, retired her Bruins jersey when she became a hockey columnist for the Toronto Star. *In addition to sports, DiManno writes on civic affairs.*

FROM ZEROES
TO HEROES

THE MAKING OF THE BIG BAD BRUINS

by Craig MacInnis

What begins a dynasty?

Contrary to myth, Bobby Orr's arrival in Beantown in the fall of 1966 did not provide instant relief for the long-suffering Bruins. Boston, who hadn't even made the playoffs since the 1958–59 season, wasn't about to let the arrival of a potential new Messiah spoil their long, and well-earned, tradition of skepticism. The pre-Orr Bruins had given their fans, and the local media, several good reasons to be wary of the club. Orr wouldn't change that — not right away and not by himself.

As far as the media were concerned, it was best to adopt a wait-and-see attitude about the 18-year-old wunderkind from Parry Sound.

"There is the . . . problem of young Orr's reaction to big league competition," *Boston Globe* reporter Tom Fitzgerald wrote on September 25, 1966, sounding a note of caution from the Bruins' training camp in London, Ontario. "[Orr] is expected to be good, but Boston hockey fans can help a lot if they contain themselves in their appraisal of the lad. They must not expect Bobby immediately will be a combination of Eddie Shore, Doug Harvey, Jack Stewart, and Dit Clapper."

In another report from London, Fitzgerald wrote, "Orr, it should be emphasized,

Orr battles Toronto's Davey Keon for the puck.

is a nice kid of 18 with a bundle of talent and a rich contract, but at the moment he's as anxious and apprehensive as any other rookie on the premises."

Of course, it didn't take long for Orr to win over the doubters. In his first exhibition game, against the Toronto Maple Leafs in London, he drew a key assist on Pit Martin's come-from-behind goal in a 1–1 tie.

By the Bruins' season home opener, a decisive 6–2 win over Gordie Howe's Detroit Red Wings, Fitzgerald was enthusing about "a brilliant debut . . . by the 18-year-old superboy, who more than fulfilled the demanding assignment by living up to all of his extravagant notices. Cheered almost every time he was on the ice, Orr stopped the show in the second period when he got an assist on a goal by Wayne Connelly. Although he did not score a goal, the lad with the blond whiffle did everything else expected of the best at his position. Bobby demonstrated that the critics who doubted his defensive savvy were dead wrong. He played the position like a veteran; was very tough in dislodging opponents around the net; blocked shots; and made adept plays in moving the puck from his own end."

Orr sent a low drive toward the net, which Connelly deflected past Wings goalie Roger Crozier, for Orr's first NHL point: "There was a truly deafening tribute after this play which lasted more than a full minute."

Appropriately, Orr's first-night opposition featured a player many felt – and still feel – was one of the greatest ever to lace on a pair of skates.

"He'll do, for sure," was Gordie Howe's post-game appraisal of the Boston rookie. Not that Howe was going to get down and genuflect after a single game. He added, "The kid's all right. He anticipates well, he makes good passes, and I guess he does just about what you'd expect of a good defenceman."

Howe, presumably, was merely being wistful when he noted that there was one big difference between Orr's arrival in the league and his own introduction to the pros two decades earlier. "Detroit gave me $250 for signing. What did they give him — $50,000?"

Less than a week later, in a losing cause against Montreal, Orr scored his first NHL goal. According to the *Boston Globe*'s report, the rookie "intercepted [Habs forward John] Ferguson's clearance just inside the blue line and fired a bullet shot on which Gump Worsley split but had no chance. For this the youngster received a standing ovation."

"It was a good shot, right about waist high," Worsley said afterwards. "I didn't see it at first but picked it up in plenty of time. But it bounced off the post into the net."

The Bruins, despite their early promise, finished in the cellar again in 1966–67. However, Orr's totals (13 goals, 41 points, in 61 games) were good enough to win the Calder Trophy for rookie of the year, despite a knee injury suffered late in the season — a portent of his injury-plagued future. He also earned a spot on the NHL's Second All-Star Team.

The Boston fans, though clearly smitten with their young star, were as jaded as ever. At the last home game of the season, a loss to Toronto, the Garden echoed to the sarcastic chant, "We are number six, We are number six."

IT WOULDN'T STAY THAT WAY FOR LONG. NOT WITH THE OFF-SEASON TRADE THAT WAS TO BRING PHIL ESPOSITO, FRED STANFIELD, AND KEN HODGE TO BOSTON FROM CHICAGO FOR GILLES MAROTTE, PIT MARTIN, AND JACK NORRIS.

Phil Esposito, Orr's great collaborator.

When analysts and pundits discuss the advent of the Big Bad Bruins, most point to the 1967–68 season, which also saw the B's add the flamboyant and pugnacious Derek Sanderson to their lineup.

In the Boston camp, the change in mood was set even before the end of the exhibition season. The occasion was a mean, fight-filled tilt with their hated rivals, the Montreal Canadiens. There were only 7,619 fans on hand at the Garden when the Bruins beat the Habs 2–1 on October 6, 1967, but the game lives on in legend as one of those watershed moments when a roster gels, when a collection of disparate players shows signs of becoming a team. Both Esposito and Hodge scored goals that night, but more importantly, the once-listless Bruins showed plenty of brute savvy.

Kevin Walsh reported in the *Boston Globe* that it took the teams "one hour to battle through the first period as 18 penalties adding up to 68 minutes were issued by referee Art Skov.

"Orr, contrary to his prevailing image as a corn-fed, painfully shy kid from the sticks, found himself in the thick of things, a willing combatant. At 11:09 [of the first period], an old rivalry was renewed as Bobby Orr and Ted Harris clashed against the boards. Orr was the big winner here as Harris ended up in the penalty box holding an ice pack to the right side of his face. The undercard at this point matched Boston rookies Glen Sather against Claude Larose and Derek Sanderson with Harris.

"But Orr wasn't finished battling. He and Bryan Watson clashed in the third period and Orr hit him with punches from every direction. This was the second major penalty of the game and earned the NHL's rookie of the year a game misconduct."

Only nine days later, the same Habs returned to Boston to open the regular season, and were trounced by the new-look Bruins, 6–2. The *Globe*'s Marvin Pave might have seen the first inkling of a future dynasty that evening. "One game doesn't make a season or, for that matter, a hockey star, but Bruins fans fell in love with a tall, rangy center named Phil Esposito last night at the Garden," wrote Pave.

"This could be the best break I've ever had," said Esposito, who notched four of the Bruins' six goals, after the game. "It's the first time I've even scored a hat trick in a National League game, and now I wind up with four."

In that transitional year of 1967–68, the injury-prone Orr skated in only 46 of the Bruins' 74 games, enough, however, to earn him a place on the NHL's First All-Star Team and to win the Norris Trophy as the league's best rearguard. (He would earn both honors in each of the next seven seasons).

But the most important thing about the campaign was that the Bruins earned a playoff spot, finishing third out of six in the new Eastern conference before bowing out in the first round to Montreal. They were doing it with Orr as their leader and with a tough, expanding nucleus that included Esposito, Hodge, Stanfield, Sanderson, Ted Green, Ed Westfall, goalie Gerry Cheevers, and veteran Johnny Bucyk, a Bruin since 1957.

The feeling around Boston, where the Bruins hadn't won since 1941, was one of mounting excitement, tempered by sensible doubt.

A key come-from-behind win against the Canadiens on December 22, 1968, vaulted the Bruins into first place for the first time in longer than anyone could remember.

In a December 23 column in the *Globe* under the headline "Purgatory over

for Bruin Fans," Ray Fitzgerald took a moment to marvel at it all. "I'm a new-comer around here. I didn't suffer through the stumbling years from 1959 to 1967, when the Bruins were lucky to beat The Little Sisters of the Poor," he began.

"But plenty of people did trudge to the Garden during those dreary seasons. They were loyal to the type of team that could win only 14 games in 70 — the record of the 1962–63 collection." Fitzgerald described the typical Boston fan as "often more belligerent than the athletes they rooted for, and better body checks were thrown in the upper balcony than on the ice.

"But the customers were loyal. They growled, but they loved the game and they loved the Bruins, bad as the team was. And above all, the customers were patient. Some day, things would be better.

"'Some day' arrived last season and reached its peak last night when the Bruins beat the Canadiens, 7–5, at the Garden to take over first place by a point."

Game by game, the Bruins of the late '60s were developing character, and a rare team chemistry that began to draw the attention of everyone, including people who didn't pay much attention to hockey.

What's more, the Bruins were as outspoken off the ice as they were surly on it. "You can intimidate those guys," Boston's Glen Sather said of the Habs. "I talk to them all the time. [Yvan] Cournoyer, all of them. I tell them they better not turn their backs on me, things like that."

But it was more than just an in-your-face attitude. The Bruins of Orr, Sanderson, and Esposito were a reflection of their times, mirroring a woolly, rock 'n' roll attitude and a brusquely assertive style that was entirely foreign to the staid old game of shinny.

Powerhouse teams before them – Punch Imlach's Leafs, say, or Toe Blake's Habs – had achieved greatness by submitting to a singular authority. The coach as martinet was a long-established recipe for success in the NHL and players that flouted the iron laws of management were usually out of town on the first bus to the minors.

But the Bruins, motivated as much by the external forces of North American pop culture as by their own obvious talent, rewrote the playbook on team comportment. If there was a sporting-world antecedent, it was probably found in the assertive flash of pro football's star quarterback of the era, the New York Jets' Joe Namath.

A November 1969 article on Sanderson and the Bruins in *Maclean's*, Canada's national magazine, began by noting that the NHL was "facing its own kind of sexual revolution, led by an irreverent, 23-year-old centre with the Boston Bruins named Derek Michael Sanderson. Sporting bell-bottom sideburns and razor-cut hair, the 176-pound Sanderson is determined to 'do his own thing' in the face of the hockey Establishment, probably the most conservative in major-league sports."

Sanderson – and I recall seeing him during this era as a junior star in Niagara Falls – was an unlikely blend of Namath, Beau Brummell, and Peter Fonda circa *Easy Rider*. The fashion dictates of the Woodstock generation figured prominently in his look (long hair, flared pants), but Sanderson was no hippie. Or if he was, he was the ironic hippie, augmenting the Peace Generation's sartorial choices with a grinning audacity that said "Get near me with that peace sign and I'll cut you."

Sanderson set himself the task of dragging the rest of the Bruins with him

SPORTS ILLUSTRATED HAD ALREADY
PICKED UP ON THE BRUINS' COUNTERCULTURE
RIFF IN AN ARTICLE ON FEBRUARY 3, 1969,
UNDER THE HEADLINE **"IT'S BOBBY ORR & THE
ANIMALS,"** REFERRING TO THE BRUINS AS
"BOSTON'S TOP ROCK GROUP," A SERVICEABLE
PUN ON THE TEAM'S POP-CULTURE PRETENSES
AND THEIR FLAMBOYANT, CHIPPY STYLE.

into the Cool Zone, building a new team standard in what might best be described as counterculture disciple. Orr was a special project.

"Orr used to have a brushcut," Sanderson told the *Maclean's* journalist, "and I told him, 'Bobby, the brushcut, forget it. It makes you look like a kid of 16.' So then I got him to a hair stylist. Now his hair is longer and it looks better, right? I told him to grow sideburns, too, but he's got no beard, so he can't grow the sideburns."

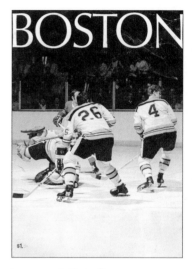

Sports Illustrated had already picked up on the Bruins' counterculture riff in an article on February 3, 1969, under the headline "It's Bobby Orr & the Animals," referring to the Bruins as "Boston's top rock group," a serviceable pun on the team's pop-culture pretenses and their flamboyant, chippy style.

Bud Poile, then general manager of the Philadelphia Flyers, said that when they "drop the puck to start the game, the Bruins think it is a piece of raw meat! Do they go after it! I'm afraid my guys will desert the place some night."

Bruins' coach Harry Sinden termed it "intimidation," while Gordie Howe, hockey's philosopher-king, reduced the Bruins' aggression to a simple human dynamic: "If you find you can push someone around, then you push him around."

Orr, it seems, was fitting nicely into the Bruins' new rock-star mold, blending aggression and superlative puck skills. "At the completion of his rush Boston fans

Opposite: *Orr with teammates Phil Esposito (left) and Johnny Bucyk.*
Inset: *A Bruins souvenir program (1970).*

scream as if he were a Beatle or a Namath," marveled writer Mark Mulvoy in *Sports Illustrated.*

Ever the paradox, Orr was championed for his deference and decency even as he gained marks as a player willing to muck it up in the corners.

"I never had a fight in my life until I came to Boston," he told *Sports Illustrated.* "Some people think fighting is terrible, but I think the odd scrap – without sticks – is part of the game."

The article also mentioned Orr's investment in a boy's camp in Orillia, Ontario, and that he owned a car wash in Toronto. On the subject of money and his big contract, he remained diplomatically tight-lipped. "Money, I don't like to talk about," he said. "I don't know what you make; I don't think you should know what I make."

Determined to turn Orr into a full-fledged sex symbol of the modern game, the magazine also noted that "Bobby dates stewardesses, models, beauty queens (like the girl from Chatham, Ontario, who waited for him outside the Detroit Olympia last week)."

As the Orr-era Bruins rolled ever closer to their date with destiny, sweeping St. Louis in four straight in May 1970, their star defenceman maintained an almost saintly aura. During the playoff run, Orr deliberately ducked the spotlight so his teammates could share in the glory. After knocking Chicago out in the semi-finals, a Toronto reporter caught up with Orr on the rubbing table in the club's infirmary, a place out of bounds to the press.

"Management won't like it if they catch you here," he told Red Burnett of the *Toronto Star.* "I'm just relaxing. Gerry Cheevers, Johnny Bucyk, Phil Esposito, and the other guys who have earned the bows are taking them out there." Coach

Harry Sinden admitted it was "a planned maneuver, a share the headlines deal." It's hard to imagine another Orr moment from that same year as being a "planned maneuver." After he scored in overtime to eliminate the Blues to win the Cup for Boston on May 10, 1970, Orr found himself in the unlikely dual role of hero and janitor.

"Forty minutes earlier Bobby Orr had scored the goal that gave Boston Bruins their first Stanley Cup in 29 years," wrote Burnett. "He had been mobbed by his teammates, chaired, kissed and hugged as he struggled to the dressing room.

"Now the hero was policing the area outside the crazy, lunatic groups that filled every inch of Bruins' dressing quarters. Ed Westfall had knocked over a trash can as he did a victory dance through the place. Orr, clutching a white terry cloth bathrobe around his dripping underwear, was picking up bottles, butts, pop cans, etc. Looking up from his chore, he said: 'I never thought there could be such a day. This is what every kid dreams of, scoring the winning goal in a Stanley Cup overtime final. Wow, I can't find words to express what I feel.'"

The reporter noted that Orr was happy, "but not too delirious to make sure his kibitzing mates didn't step on a bottle or jagged can with their bare feet."

And so this is how the Bruins' big, bad drive to the Cup ended: with their superstar quietly picking up the trash, and with their fans flooding the streets of Boston in quiet ecstasy.

A cop outside the Garden, faced with the prospect of an impromptu parade in the seething streets of the city's north end, hardly seem fazed. "We don't even have our riot helmets," the cop said into his walkie-talkie. "No, no, don't send them. We won't need them for this crowd. These people aren't protesting anything."

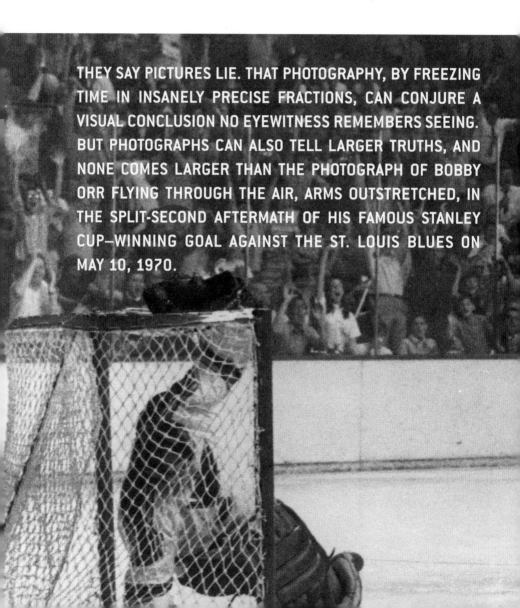

SNAPSHOT OF

THEY SAY PICTURES LIE. THAT PHOTOGRAPHY, BY FREEZING TIME IN INSANELY PRECISE FRACTIONS, CAN CONJURE A VISUAL CONCLUSION NO EYEWITNESS REMEMBERS SEEING. BUT PHOTOGRAPHS CAN ALSO TELL LARGER TRUTHS, AND NONE COMES LARGER THAN THE PHOTOGRAPH OF BOBBY ORR FLYING THROUGH THE AIR, ARMS OUTSTRETCHED, IN THE SPLIT-SECOND AFTERMATH OF HIS FAMOUS STANLEY CUP–WINNING GOAL AGAINST THE ST. LOUIS BLUES ON MAY 10, 1970.

It is the image of the sporting hero as Superman, as a winged deity taking flight while his earthbound adversaries (goalie Glenn Hall, defenceman Noel Picard) huddle in bleak resignation.

Nearly 30 years later, it remains the sport's defining image. Not because it encapsulates the thrill of victory and agony of defeat, which it does, but because it offers the essential visual pun on Orr's career: the guy "raised his game" to a superhuman level.

Sure, everyone had always known it, but here, forever, was the proof that Orr (rhymes with soar) had his cosmic pilot's license, authorized to deliver the cellar-dwelling Bruins to uncharted heights.

Boston had not won the Cup in 29 years when Orr fired his overtime marker to win the game and sweep the series in four straight. And the recollection of it gave Orr's teammate Derek Sanderson the chance to wax poetic.

"Did you see the way he gambled to start that play?" Sanderson asked a journalist after the game. "No other defenceman would have risked so much in an overtime game. But for Orr, with his natural talent and great anticipation, it was no gamble.

"Their man played it right, tried to dump the puck past Orr for a breakaway. Bobby trapped the puck, fed it to me, I moved around the backboards until he floated into position and then fed it to him.

"I knew it was all over when the puck left his stick. You can't stop a laser beam."

— Craig MacInnis

Orr takes flight after scoring his Cup-winning goal.

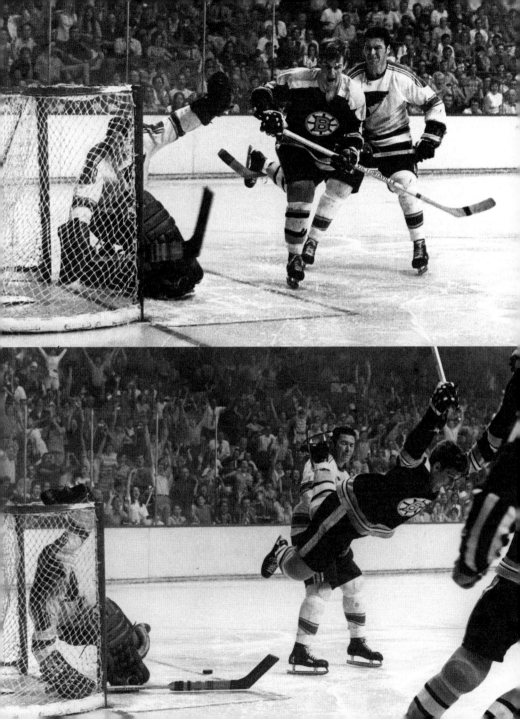

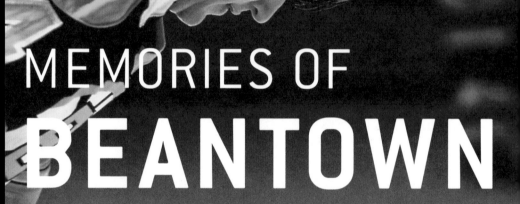

MEMORIES OF
BEANTOWN

REMEMBERING BOBBY'S LEGACY

by Jonathan Kahn

The 1970s were a vexing time in Boston. Its influence as a commercial centre had long since waned, as industry fled south. The legacy of "the best and the brightest" was a distant memory; the Kennedy mystique was in decline, felled by bullets and Chappaquiddick. Boston was no longer on the front pages as a political or cultural hub, but rather as a city torn by racial strife and busing. In sports, too, Boston found itself in decline.

But Boston had been given Bobby Orr. And Kevin was not going to let anyone forget it.

Kevin, my neighbour in my sophomore year, was insane. How else to describe an 18-year-old who spontaneously, uncontrollably, and completely out of context, would scream "Number four, Bobby Orr!!" at the top of his lungs?

I was 17 when I moved to Boston for my first year of college, fresh from a Montreal high school career punctuated by annual Stanley Cup parades down Ste. Catherine Street. It was bad enough that I had to slum it watching the likes of Stan Jonathon and John Wensink after cutting my teeth on Beliveau and Cournoyer and Lafleur. It was bad enough that I had to trade the majesty of the Forum for the rat-infested Boston Garden (complete with streetcar tracks running across its roof). But I really saw no need to suffer through these bizarre and apparently heartfelt bursts – pronounced more like "Numbah fo-ah, Bahby o-ah!" – emanating from next door.

Even college students, who happily accepted all manner of habits and activities from roommates and neighbours in those pre-Ronald Reagan/young college conservatives years, found this particular act tough to understand.

Kevin's eruptions seemed to occur regardless of whether the Bruins happened to be on TV at the time. They occurred even though Bobby Orr was at that point a retired member of the Chicago Blackhawks. (Oh, how I loved to rub that little bit of Blackhawk salt into Kevin's Bruins wounds.) Too much time in suburbia and not enough time spent on dates might begin to explain such behavior, but Kevin's case was special. He set his wristwatch alarm for 4:44. He would remind the casual listener that the name Ray Bourque was really pronounced B-orr-que – get it? Not coincidence, but divine revelation. Kevin would bring a radio with him on Bruin game nights and blurt out "Numbah fo-ah, Bahby o-ah" when the Bruins scored, which could be embarrassing if you were at a restaurant or a Bruce Springsteen concert at the time.

I am told by reliable sources that, some years later, Kevin could be found floating the "Numbah fo-ah" mantra in the direction of his wife's pregnant belly in the hopes of properly initiating the little Bruin fanatic to be.

The Celtics could play the Garden (or, in the local parlance, the "Gahden") in the afternoon followed by a Bruins game in the evening, and the stands would register a 100 percent turnover – not one fan in common. The Celtics were class and money and style and suburbs. The Bruins were lunch buckets and beer and toughness, on and off the ice. Remember those brawls between visiting teams and Bruins fans? You never saw that at Celtic games. Ask a Bruins supporter how the

game went and you might be told, "Awesome – you should have seen Wensink kick butt in that fight . . ." The Celtics were about intelligent play; their soul was Cowens and Havlicek, later Bird and McHale. The Big Bad Bruins were about Ted Green and Pie McKenzie and Wayne Cashman and Terry O'Reilly and John Wensink. What was a white-collar hockey fan to do? Cling to Orr. You might like O'Reilly, but you could feel pride in Orr.

And frankly, it was hard to feel proud as a Boston sports fan in the late 1970s. As was the case in other matters, these were vexing times. The memories of the glorious close call of 1975, personified by Carlton Fisk, had been overtaken by the nightmare close call of 1978, personified by Bucky Dent and that villain for all time, Mike Torrez. John Havlicek was gone, Larry Bird was still a college player in Indiana, and shockingly the Celtics dynasty was in the cellar. The Patriots were, well, the Patriots.

THE BRUINS WERE STILL GOOD, TO BE FAIR. BUT ORR WAS GONE . . . AS WERE ESPO, BUCYK, AND MOST OF THE REST.

The glories of 1972 were increasingly distant, and 1970 even more so. The legacy of Bobby Orr, lateral in flight, arms raised in victory, puck nestled behind a dejected Glenn Hall, was preserved in the ubiquitous (at least in Boston) poster.

But the feasts of the past made a poor meal for the present. The Celtics were always expected to win. The Red Sox were destined to come close only to run

Briefly a Black Hawk: Orr helps goalie
Tony Esposito defend the Chicago net.

tragically into the Curse, as the trade of Babe Ruth and the resulting near-century of heartbreak was known (see Bob Gibson and Bucky Dent and, later, Bill Buckner). But before Orr, the Bruins' role in the grand hockey scheme had always been to finish last, and badly.

They were the Washington Generals to the Globetrotters of Montreal, Toronto, and Detroit. Then along came Orr, a fantastically talented offensive and defensive force, who, in the process of revolutionizing the way the game was played, transformed the sad-sack Bruins into Stanley Cup champions.

ORR WAS MORE LIKE A CELTIC THAN A BRUIN — CLASS, SKILL, SPEED, VISION.

But he became more than that. Orr gave Boston something it had seldom if ever had before and has not had since, a national figure, the undisputed giant of his sport. He was bigger than Havlicek, than Cowens, bigger even than Auerbach. Bigger than Lynn and Rice and Fisk and bigger than the local institution known as Yaz. These were local heroes.

Most of Boston's top stars had shadows to box. When there was Russell, there was Chamberlain, just as years later Bird's legend was inevitably harnessed to Magic Johnson's. Williams came close but there was always this small matter of DiMaggio, and when DiMaggio retired he was replaced by another centrefielder, this one named Mantle. But in the National Hockey League between 1968 and 1974, there was no doubt who reigned — Orr. He could be mentioned, and still is, in the same breath as Richard, as Chamberlain, as Gehrig, and as that hefty ballplayer who got away.

And in Boston, that resonated. Kennedy, it was then felt, had shown class and skill and had exuded a kind of magic. To see him replaced by a rancher from Texas, a weirdo from California, and a peanut farmer from Georgia was galling. The Republican revolution was coming and the last local political hero, Tip O'Neill, was soon to fade. But Orr was still the greatest. His replacements at the pinnacle of his sport, Lafleur and Dionne and Bossy, were great, but they were not Orr.

Orr raised the game of those around him. He also lifted the spirits of Boston fans, who, for the first time in decades, could feel part of a winning tradition. No, check that. With Orr, Boston found a link to magic, to a sports-world version of the Kennedy mystique.

And Kevin? He's still a Bruins fanatic. He ended up working in the bio-tech industry that sprung from the ashes of Boston's old manufacturing core. He got his first job the same year that Edmonton, led by a brilliant young superstar out of Brantford, won its first Stanley Cup.

Jonathan Kahn, an unreconstructed Canadiens fan, spent his formative years in the sports cauldron of late '70s Boston. He currently practises law in Toronto.

RATING

ORR

HOW GREAT WAS HE?

by Frank Orr

Even the hyperbole about Bobby Orr, the exaggerations to illuminate points on his greatness, set him apart from other defencemen and all but a very few hockey players at any position. Not even the myths that surrounded other greats matched Orr's.

Was he quick?

"One time Orr shot the puck from the point and got to the front of the net in time to deflect his own shot, at least, I think I saw it," said Tom Johnson, Hall-of-Fame defenceman and a long-time Bruin executive and coach for two seasons.

Did Orr "see" the game differently than others, say, in slow motion, to give him a unique view of the play?

"I suppose he did," said Harry Sinden, Bruin coach from Orr's entry in 1966 to the 1970 Cup win and the team's long-time general manager. "But how could you know? No one ever saw it his way and reacted to what he saw the way Orr did so I suppose he had some different view of it. Maybe Wayne Gretzky or Mario Lemieux, who seemed to have that quality, could explain it, although I doubt it. None of them think about it; they just do it."

Was Orr fast, especially when his knees were still even reasonably good?

"I doubt we ever saw his top speed because he was as fast as he needed to

At the 21st NHL All-Star Game, January 16, 1968, wearing #5. Jean Beliveau wore Orr's #4.

be in a particular situation," said Phil Esposito, the great Bruin centre and partner with Orr in a devastating offense.

"No matter how fast an opponent was, Bobby could skate faster than him if he needed to do it in the framework of a play. If he was caught up the ice and the other team had an odd-man rush, that's when you saw his truly great speed. Very seldom did he not get back to have a hand in breaking up the play. To have seen his ultimate speed would have needed a play faster than any in hockey history."

How about Orr's ability to anticipate how a play would form and react to it at such an early point that there seemed to be no rhyme or reason to what he was doing?

"WE USED TO KID HIM ABOUT HIS ANTICIPATION, TELL HIM IF HE REALLY CONCENTRATED ON IT HE COULD TELL US WHAT WOULD HAPPEN AT THE 11:55 MARK OF THE SECOND PERIOD IN A GAME NEXT WEEK," SAID BRUIN GOALIE GERRY CHEEVERS.

In rating the game's great defencemen and where Orr fits on the list, first we must establish categories. Various polls of those who have watched the game for a long time place three men in the top flight - Orr, Doug Harvey, and Eddie Shore.

The second plateau of backliners includes King Clancy, Ray Bourque, Denis Potvin, Larry Robinson, Paul Coffey, Chris Chelios, Tim Horton, Brad Park, Red Kelly, and Dit Clapper.

Kelly and Clapper had double roles. Kelly was a First Team All-Star defencemen when the Detroit Red Wings won four Stanley Cup titles, then a top centre when the Toronto Maple Leafs won four times. Clapper started as a Bruin right winger, twice a Second Team All-Star, then switched to defence where he was a

Hometown hero: Orr returns to Parry Sound,
chauffeured by brother Ron in 1967 (top), and
honoured at "Bobby Orr Day" in 1970 (bottom).

ORR'S REVOLUTIONARY APPROACH OPENED THE DOOR
FOR THE BEST OFFENSIVE DEFENCEMEN WHO FOLLOWED
— PARK, POTVIN, ROBINSON, GUY LAPOINTE, BORJE
SALMING, LARRY MURPHY, BOURQUE, COFFEY, CHELIOS,
BRIAN LEETCH.

First Team All-Star three times, the only player to qualify for the All-Star team as both a forward and a defenceman.

Remove durability from the list of attributes. What sets Orr apart from this splendid, talented herd is that on any list rating the skills that made players exceptional, he is at the top of just about all tabulations.

Of course, a Black Jack Stewart or Bob Baun were better bodycheckers; Sprague Cleghorn, Shore, or Potvin had a wider mean streak; Jimmy Thomson, Bob Goldham, Hap Day, or Lionel Hitchman were superior in the tactics of pure defensive hockey.

But Orr was better in what those qualities produced by different methods. He did not have to knock people down because he was so fast that he could stay between any foe and where that attacker wanted to go. While Orr could fight superbly and apply the lumber to opposition bodies, he intimidated with what he might do if he got the puck. Knocks that he was not a great defensive player, of course, were a laugh, criticism concocted by those who would turn down Kim Basinger because she had a zit. Orr could play strong defence when necessary but the "Orr of coaches," Scotty Bowman, once guffawed at a suggestion that #4 was weak when the opposition had the puck.

"A few people knocked Orr and Gretzky and Guy Lafleur as being ineffective defensively, which made me just shake my head," Bowman said. "When my teams played against Orr and Gretzky — and Lafleur was on my side — much of the time when they were on the ice, they had the puck. It's difficult for the opposition to score in that situation and that seems like rather good defence to me. And if they didn't have the puck, they were the best at stripping it from the opposition."

Orr fights off New York Ranger Arnie Brown.

The idea of Orr as a weak defensive player is scuttled by his play in the 1970–71 season. He finished the schedule a record plus-124, on the ice for 179 Bruins goals, and only 55 goals against in equal manpower situations. Only a plus-120 by Robinson approaches Orr's number.

That Orr changed the game as much as any player in history leads to some debate. Jacques Plante's safaris out of the net to block shoot-ins at the backboards and his clearing passes altered the goalie's role enormously. Gretzky's "office," the area behind the net where he would hold the puck before making a play, was a major new twist. In the '40s, the Detroit Red Wings installed the shoot-and-chase to counter the Toronto Maple Leafs four-man defensive wall at the blueline, which was used to combat the original rush attacks by the Wings' great Production Line of Syd Abel, Gordie Howe, and Ted Lindsay (but especially the young Howe).

There were fine offensive defencemen, too, before Orr arrived – Clancy and Shore in the '30s, Babe Pratt and Flash Hollett in the '40s, Kelly and Harvey in the '50s, Pierre Pilote in the '60s. They contributed by originating attacks with quick outlet passes, then following the play. As time moved along, the rusher's role in the attack increased. Pratt rushed much more than Shore did, Harvey was up the ice more than Pratt, and Pilote was involved in offence more than Harvey. But along came Orr and the boundaries for the rushing defenceman disappeared. Perhaps the style of pre-1911 hockey, when the seven-man game included the rover, best mirrors Orr's ability, and gives us a player who compares accurately to Orr. Fred "Cyclone" Taylor, a fabled performer in the pre-NHL days, was a rover and later a defenceman who went anywhere on the ice, as long as he could be effective. Taylor was moved back to defence because the other forwards could not

keep pace with him. When Orr arrived in '66, some observed, not all tongue-in-cheek, that the rover was restored to the game.

"When Bobby joined us, there was a strong outlook around the NHL that he would be forced to make a big change from the game he played in junior to be effective in the big league," Sinden said. "I actually was asked how difficult it was going to be to put the halter on him and work him into a system of play if we were going to do anything as a team.

"As it turned out, the problem was the exact reverse of that — to get our other players to enlarge their games to augment the way Bobby played.

"Actually, Orr played a very simple, basic game. But he played it at a level so superior to anyone else's that sometimes he had to tone it down or he would have been on the ice by himself, with no one to perform even close to his level."

Any idea that a defenceman could lead the NHL in scoring seemed absurd,

Orr confers with bench boss Harry Sinden.

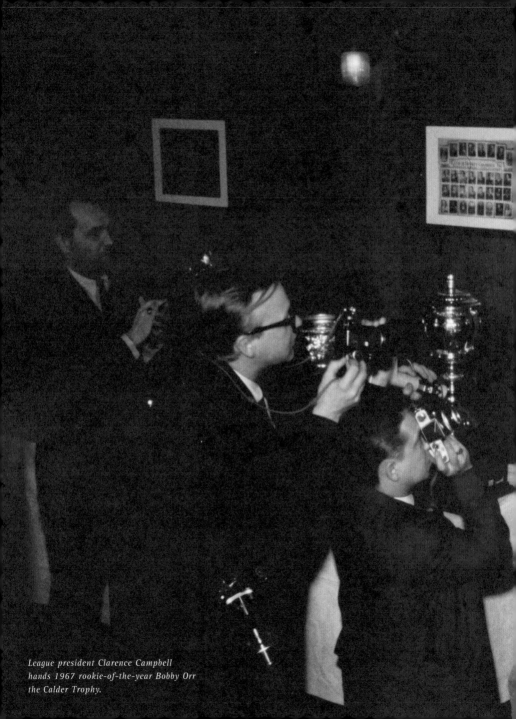

League president Clarence Campbell hands 1967 rookie-of-the-year Bobby Orr the Calder Trophy.

SEVERAL DEFENCEMEN HAVE PASSED ORR'S CAREER POINT TOTALS BECAUSE OF THEIR LONGEVITY **BUT NONE HAVE THREATENED HIS MARK OF 1.39 POINTS PER GAME DURING THE REGULAR SEASON, 1.24 IN THE PLAYOFFS.**

equivalent to, as one writer put it, "a pitcher leading major league baseball in home runs," which brings to mind the feats of an earlier Boston legend, Babe Ruth. But in the 1969–70 season, Orr did exactly that, winning the scoring title with 120 points, 21 points more than runner-up Esposito. To show this was no freak occurrence, Orr was second in scoring three times, third once to Esposito, before adding another title in 1974–75.

Orr's revolutionary approach opened the door for the best offensive defencemen who followed – Park, Potvin, Robinson, Guy Lapointe, Borje Salming, Larry Murphy, Bourque, Coffey, Chelios, Brian Leetch.

Several defencemen passed Orr's career point totals because of their longevity but none have threatened his mark of 1.39 points per game during the regular season, 1.24 in the playoffs.

Doug Harvey was the best ever at controlling the pace of a game. Appearing to be half asleep, Harvey would take the puck and, almost walking, not skating, would move around the Canadiens zone with it until the opposition was befuddled and out of position. When Harvey had slowed the pace to a standstill, a Canadiens forward would break, Harvey would place one of those soft, deadly accurate passes on his tape, and the offence was launched.

"Harvey could play the game in a rocking chair and be effective," said Frank Selke, the genius GM who built the post-war Montreal powerhouse organization.

Tom Johnson was Harvey's teammate and biggest admirer. "Doug did not carry the puck all that much but he would get it in our zone and drift with it," Johnson said. "Often that lured an opposition winger or two into our end and he would trap them with a pass."

Much of the time Orr did not come around his own net at full speed and

The Canadiens' Jacques Laperriere chases Orr for the puck.

head up ice with the puck, the way Coffey and Leetch do so well. He would skate slowly out of the Bruins' zone, then light his jets at neutral ice, speeding up in a stride.

"Harvey was extraordinary but Bobby was quicker, quicker than anyone I ever saw," Johnson said. "Bobby set the pace of the game by taking things to top speed. And he had that move."

Orr's signature manoeuvre was the pivot, a 360-degree turn at high speed to elude a checker. He also had a 45-degree turn, and his lateral movement was unusual.

"Bobby would be coming at you one-on-one and, all of sudden, he would be eight or ten feet on either side of his original path for no obvious reason, a little spooky, in fact," said Serge Savard, a splendid defenceman himself whose move inspired Montreal broadcaster Danny Gallivan's famous phrase "Savardian spinorama."

Orr changed the defenceman's game, but the changes in the game Orr inspired off the ice were of an even greater magnitude than his influence when wearing his skates. With now-disgraced lawyer Alan Eagleson as his agent, Orr signed his first pro contract with the Bruins in '66, a deal that gave him a $25,000 per season salary and a signing bonus of at least $20,000. The best previous rookie deal was $8,000 per season.

With Orr and Bruins goalie Ed Johnston as main backers, Eagleson was able to form the first NHL Players' Association and make it stick with the owners, who had scuttled a similar attempt a decade earlier.

When the NHL expanded by six teams in '67, the desire to see Orr brought fans to the new buildings and introduced them to the game. Orr steadily pushed

salaries upwards, becoming the first player to earn $200,000 a season in '71. Then in '76, Orr was the first free agent in NHL history to change teams with no compensation to his previous club when he left the Bruins after a bitter contract dispute and moved to the Chicago Blackhawks.

But his knees were gone by then and after a wonderful last hurrah, leading Team Canada to victory in the '76 Canada Cup, including a win over the Russians (Orr had missed the historic '72 Summit Series because of knee woes), he played only 26 games for the Hawks over three seasons, missing all of 1977–78, then retired.

ORR DEPARTED AS GOOD A PLAYER AS ANYONE WHO EVER PLAYED THE GAME, LIKELY BETTER, BUT LEAVING A NAGGING QUESTION: HOW GOOD WOULD HE HAVE BEEN WITH TWO SOUND KNEES FOR HIS ENTIRE CAREER?

Veteran sportswriter Frank Orr (no relation) was inducted into the Hockey Hall of Fame in 1989. As a reporter and columnist with the Toronto Star, *he covered Orr during his junior days in Oshawa and as an NHL star with the Bruins and Team Canada.*

Orr's #4 gets a hero's hoist in a ceremony at Boston Garden in 1979.

CHERRY
ON ORR

AN INTERVIEW WITH DON CHERRY

by Craig MacInnis

There is no greater keeper of Bobby Orr's legend than his coach and longtime friend Don Cherry, who guided the Bruins in the mid-'70s during Orr's last great years in Beantown.

Cherry is best known these days for his cuffs-up commentary on "Coach's Corner," the first-intermission mainstay of CBC's *Hockey Night in Canada*. He recently took time to reminisce about "the greatest player ever."

ON SEEING ORR FOR THE FIRST TIME

I was playing for the Rochester Americans and we were into Boston to play that night. Boston was practising that morning, and I'd seen him on TV but when I walked up to the glass and saw him practise, I couldn't believe it – and this is from a guy that's been to every camp of the Original Six for a cup of coffee! I'd seen them all – Gordie, Rocket, Bobby Hull, the whole deal.

I even thought so much of it I went down to the Boston Bruin pro shop and got a poster and had [Rochester teammate] Bob Walton give it to [Orr's teammate] Mike Walton to go in and sign it for me for my son Tim.

I'd never seen anything like it, and he was the best hockey player and I have

Don Cherry, Canada's most flamboyant and outspoken hockey voice.

to laugh when people say 'Compare him to other hockey players.' I think Bobby Clarke said it best. He said, 'Too bad they don't have another league for him to go to. He's too good for the NHL.'

Serge Savard said, "There's stars, superstars, and then there's Bobby Orr."

ON ORR WINNING THE SCORING CHAMPIONSHIP WITH CHERRY BEHIND THE BENCH

He had 46 goals, 89 assists, and was plus-128. The guy who'll win it this year will probably be about plus-52 or plus-60. And I saw him pass up goals and points because we were playing expansion teams. Once we'd get up 4–1 or 5–1 he would not want to embarrass the other teams and he would not try to put a million goals behind 'em, either.

He was very, very shy after he'd score a goal. After a great goal, he'd put his head down. He felt embarrassed for the other team.

ON ORR'S GREATEST ON-ICE FEATS

A lot of people don't realize that he used to block shots and he was a tremendous hitter and he used to fight. You have a lot of superstars in the league that can get a lot of goals, as you know. But they sure don't block shots. He did it all.

Possibly the greatest goal I ever saw, there's two of them they talk about. There was one in Oakland where he was killing a penalty and lost his glove at centre ice somehow, so he skated backwards with the puck and as he went by his glove, he put his glove on, turned around, and put on the burners, went in on [Oakland goalie] Gary Smith, shot the puck, which the goalie juggled and it went

Orr in his classic shot-blocking stance.

"A LOT OF PEOPLE DON'T REALIZE THAT HE USED TO **BLOCK SHOTS** AND HE WAS A **TREMENDOUS HITTER** AND HE USED TO **FIGHT.**"

into the air. And as Bobby went by the net, he hit the puck and it went into the top corner.

Then there was one against the Flames where he was killing a penalty. You couldn't chase him behind the net, eh? Because if you chased him behind the net he'd just come out the other side and he'd just go around and around.

So, the Flames did not chase him, so Orr came down the right side very slowly – they didn't want to rush at him – went over their blueline, went into their corner and for some reason, I still don't know why, they all rushed him, including the goaltender. The goalie tried to stop him from going behind the net, right? He fell down, Bobby came out and backhanded it into the open net and there were all the players laying on the ice. He looked back and put his stick on his knees and put his head down, because he'd embarrassed the other team.

HOW ORR SHAPES UP AGAINST THE OTHER GREATS OF THE GAME

I'M NOT PUTTING DOWN DOUG HARVEY BUT DOUG HARVEY NEVER GOT 46 GOALS AND HE NEVER GOT 89 ASSISTS, AND NEITHER DID EDDIE SHORE.

I saw Doug Harvey play and I played for Shore, but I never saw him play. But for just sheer excitement of watching the guy on the ice, not only was he getting all the points but he was just a joy to watch. When I first saw him, it was like an old horse trainer who finally saw Secretariat.

Half-hearted clinch: Orr and the Leafs' Jim Pappin perform a gentle pas de deux.

ON ORR'S NAGGING KNEE INJURIES

He used to "leave his leg" as they say. And my brother Dick who was at camp with him when he was a rookie said, 'He's gonna get hurt because he takes too many chances and he's too young [18] to be going into the National Hockey League,' and that's exactly what happened, he got hurt.

Why everybody thinks Bobby is still great is the last [full] year he played for me [1974-75] he got 46 goals, 89 assists, and then he went to Team Canada [in the 1976 Canada Cup] and was picked the Most Valuable Player — and nobody ever saw him play again! He went to Chicago and that was it. Nobody ever saw him play in Chicago, so everybody remembers him winning the scoring title and the Canada Cup MVP.

ON THE MYSTIQUE OF THE BOSTON BRUINS DURING ORR'S REIGN

When I first went into the Garden and it was quiet I could almost see him with the puck. I hate to say it, the Lord might be mad at me, but when he first went there they called him "Moses" that he was going to lead them out of the bull rushes because they hadn't made the playoffs. Then a couple of years later they called him "God," so the players absolutely revered him.

Let's face it, he was the guy they all had good years with. I'm not going to start naming players, but what happened was, players after he left never had theyears they had when he was there, so he made the Bruins.

"AND MY BROTHER DICK WHO WAS AT CAMP WITH HIM WHEN HE WAS A ROOKIE SAID, **'HE'S GONNA GET HURT BECAUSE HE TAKES TOO MANY CHANCES AND HE'S TOO YOUNG [18] TO BE GOING INTO THE NATIONAL HOCKEY LEAGUE,'** AND THAT'S EXACTLY WHAT HAPPENED, HE GOT HURT."

"I REMEMBER ONE TIME HE SAID TO ME WHEN I WAS GIVING THE TEAM HECK — THIS IS A TRUE STORY! — HE CAME TO ME AND SAID, 'DON, DO YOU THINK WHEN YOU'RE GIVING THE TEAM HECK YOU CAN GIVE ME HECK A LITTLE, TOO?'"

ON ORR'S ON-ICE TEMPERAMENT

A very mean streak. He used to fight, a lot of people don't realize that. He fought Teddy Harris and knocked him cold. He used to fight a lot. He had a real mean streak.

I remember one time there was a minute to go in a game in L.A., he grabbed one of our players and pulled him off the ice. Orr jumped on the ice and grabbed this guy and got in a fight with him. After, I asked him why. He said, "He was laughing at us." They were beating us and he was laughing at us so Bobby's temper got a hold of him.

ON ORR'S LEADERSHIP

I remember one time he said to me when I was giving the team heck - this is a true story! – he came to me and said, "Don, do you think when you're giving the team heck you can give me heck a little, too?"

It was hard to do. I didn't tell him much. He wanted to play all the time. He'd play hurt. One thing you had to watch was he'd play hurt. You'd have to keep him off morning skates a lot cause he wanted to be with the guys. But there was no way I was going to tell Bobby Orr how to play. "Jump over the boards!"

ON ORR REVOLUTIONIZING THE ROLE OF THE DEFENCEMAN

He changed how defence should be played. Paul Coffey, Phil Housley, you go down the list. He broke the mold because before that defencemen were big,

"HE CHANGED THE WHOLE FACE OF THE GAME AND HOW IT'S PLAYED."

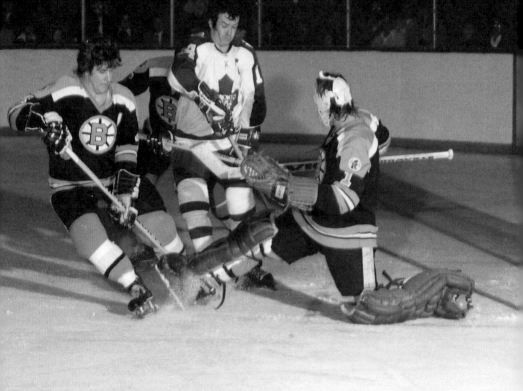

slow guys. They just cleared the guys out and got the puck up. He changed the whole face of the game and how it's played.

ON ORR'S LASTING INFLUENCE:

Bobby does commercials and I don't think that has anything to do with it. There's somehow or other a mystique about him, and I think it's because he played for the Bruins. The Bruins, of the Original Six in the States, they seem to be the glamour team, or were the glamour team back then. And the name, Big Bad Bruins. That started before I got there. They weren't really the 'bad' Bruins. They were the Big Good Bruins. When I got there they got to be the Big Bad Bruins; there was no team tougher than those guys.

ON THE BOSTON GARDEN DURING ORR'S YEARS

It was unbelievable. It was like the fans would tap you on the shoulder and tell you what to do. You could hear a guy just talking normal up in the Gallery Gods, y'know? It was like so intimate, and it went straight up and down, almost, the seats. It was like the crowd was part of the game. It was just a great atmosphere. Of all the buildings, that and Chicago were the best.

The Boston fan, in the States, is the most knowledgeable fan, because they've been there since the 1920s. Generation after generation after generation goes. Half the people are still there from when I went, and they still keep going. That and Detroit, but even more so than Detroit, they're the most knowledgeable fans. They consider themselves Canadians.

In the Bruins den: the Leafs' Davey Keon battles Orr and Bruins goalie Gilles Gilbert.

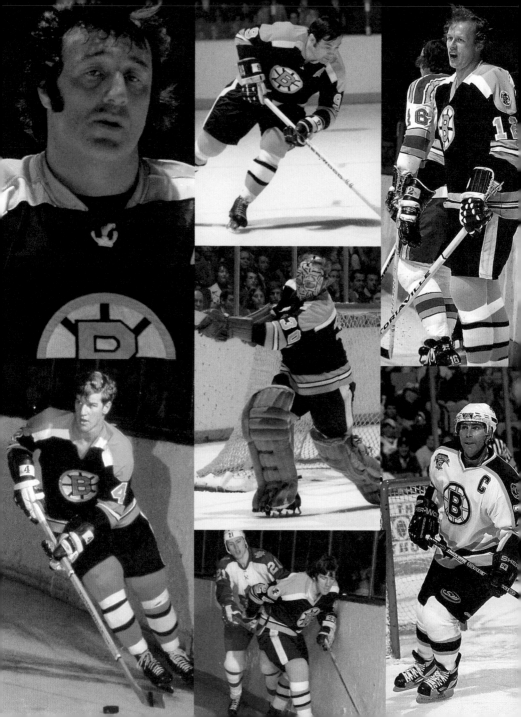

If you go around here, especially in the East, in the Maritimes, you'll see more Boston Bruins sweaters than you will any other sweater from the Original Six teams from the States.

ON CURRENT PLAYERS WHO RESEMBLE ORR

I can't think of one guy that skates like him, is tough like him, and scores like him. I think up front the closest thing I saw to him was Cam Neely. Cam could do it all. Fifty goals. Fight, hit, block shots. He was a forward, I know, but there's nobody, I feel, that did the same thing as Bobby.

ON CHERRY'S ALL-TIME BRUINS DREAM TEAM

I WOULD HAVE TO HAVE CHEEVERS IN NET AND YOU'D HAVE TO HAVE PHIL [ESPOSITO], YOU'D HAVE TO HAVE BUCYK, NOBODY TALKS ABOUT HIS 500 GOALS. YOU'D HAVE TO HAVE TERRY O'REILLY AND CASHMAN ON RIGHT WING, AND THE OTHER DEFENCEMAN YOU'D HAVE TO HAVE WITH ORR IS BOURQUE.

THAT'D BE MY ALL-STARS, AND ME BEHIND THE BENCH.

Don Cherry's Bruin Dream Team (clockwise from left): Esposito, Bucyk, Cashman, Bourque, O'Reilly, Orr, and Cheevers (centre).

WHAT THEY

"WHY DID LARRY BIRD, DURING NATIONAL ANTHEMS, LOOK UP AT THE BOSTON GARDEN CEILING? NO ONE KNEW UNTIL A NIGHT IN 1988 WHEN LARRY BIRD EXPLAINED TO AN AUDIENCE THAT INCLUDED BOBBY ORR THAT WHAT HE WAS DOING WAS LOOKING AT BOBBY ORR'S RETIRED NUMBER 4."

— *Bob Ryan, Boston Globe*

"YOU MEET PEOPLE NOW WHO SAY, 'I HAVEN'T GONE TO A GAME SINCE ORR LEFT.'"

— *Fred Cusick, former Bruins play-by-play announcer*

"I LIKE TO CALL THEM THE HOCKEY TRINITY — GRETZKY BEING THE SON, HOWE BEING THE FATHER, AND BOBBY ORR LIKE THE HOLY GHOST, BECAUSE HE WAS TRULY AMAZING."

— *Bob McKenzie, Hockey News*

"AS THE NO. 1 ATTRACTION IN THE GAME TODAY, YOUNG MR. ORR FIGURES TO CAUSE A WAVE OF INSOMNIA AMONG RIVAL

SAID

COACHES. HOW DO THEY PREVENT HIM FROM MAKING THEIR ANTELOPE LOOK LIKE WATER BUFFALO WITH A TOUCH OF HEPATITIS?"

— *Milt Dunnell, Toronto Star*

"IF THERE WERE TWO DOZEN BOBBY ORRS IN THIS LEAGUE, WE'D HAVE TO ERECT BUILDINGS THAT WOULD HOLD 60,000."

— *Milt Schmidt, former Bruin general manager*

"HE MAKES THE GAME LOOK SO EASY THAT IT'S ALMOST DISCOURAGING."

— *Ken Hodge, Orr's teammate*

"I WOULD SAY I'VE NEVER SEEN A GUY WHO DID AS MUCH OFFENSIVELY AND DEFENSIVELY AS MUCH AS THAT YOUNG MAN DID."

— *Gordie Howe*

"I'VE SEEN ALL THE GREATS SINCE THE 1920S, AND I'VE NEVER SEEN A PLAYER WITH THE SKILLS OF ORR."

— *Clarence Campbell, former NHL president*

"I KNOW WHAT HE DOES TO A TEAM BECAUSE I EXPERIENCED IT WHEN WE PLAYED TOGETHER IN THE CANADA CUP. WE WERE LIKE A BUNCH OF KIDS ON A POND WAITING FOR SOMEONE TO COME ALONG AND ORGANIZE US. WHEN HE WALKED IN THE ROOM, WE KNEW WE WOULD BE ALL RIGHT."

— *Denis Potvin, former New York Islanders defenceman*

"IF BOBBY ORR HAS A PROBLEM, IT'S JUST THAT HE HAS NO FEAR. IF NOTHING ELSE WILL DO, I SWEAR HE'LL USE HIS HEAD TO BLOCK A SHOT."

— *Gerry Cheevers, Bruins goalie*

"I'D GIVE HIM MY KNEES IF IT WOULD HELP HIM PLAY AGAIN."

—*Don Awrey, former Bruin*

"WHAT WAS SO SPECIAL ABOUT HIM? EVERYTHING. JUST THAT HE WAS SKATING RINGS AROUND EVERYONE ELSE."

— *Wren Blair, Bruins scout who discovered Orr at age 12 in a tournament in Gananoque, Ontario*

"I REMEMBER HAP EMMS SAYING [ORR] WILL NEVER MAKE IT TO THE NHL — HE'S NOT BIG ENOUGH AND NEVER WILL BE."

— *Eddie Westfall, Bruins forward, recalling a prediction by the legendary Niagara Falls junior coach*

"WE HATED TO CHECK HIM. WE RESPECT HIM SO MUCH THAT WE DON'T WANT TO DO ANYTHING TO DAMAGE THOSE KNEES."

— *Richard Mulhern, Atlanta Flames defenceman*

"BOBBY ORR WAS A STAR WHEN THEY PLAYED THE NATIONAL ANTHEM IN HIS FIRST GAME."

— *Harry Sinden, Bruins general manager*

BOBBY ORR

REGULAR SEASON **ONTARIO HOCKEY ASSN.**

YEAR	TEAM	GP	G	A	PTS	PIM
1962–63	Oshawa Generals	34	6	15	21	45
1963–64	Oshawa Generals	56	29	43	72	142
1964–65	Oshawa Generals	55	34	59	93	112
1965–66	Oshawa Generals	47	38	56	94	92
TOTALS		192	107	173	280	391
PLAYOFF TOTALS		29	09	32	41	45

REGULAR SEASON **NATIONAL HOCKEY LEAGUE**

YEAR	TEAM	GP	G	A	PTS	PIM
1966–67	Boston Bruins	61	13	28	41	102
1967–68	Boston Bruins	46	11	20	31	63
1968–69	Boston Bruins	67	21	43	64	133
1969–70	Boston Bruins	76	33	87	120	125
1970–71	Boston Bruins	78	37	102	139	91
1971–72	Boston Bruins	76	37	80	117	106
1972–73	Boston Bruins	63	29	72	101	99
1973–74	Boston Bruins	74	32	90	122	82
1974–75	Boston Bruins	80	46	89	135	101
1975–76	Boston Bruins	10	05	13	18	22
1976–77	Chi. Black Hawks	20	04	19	23	25
1977–78	Chi. Black Hawks			(DID NOT PLAY)		
1978–79	Chi. Black Hawks	06	02	02	04	04
TOTALS		657	270	645	915	953
PLAYOFF TOTALS		74	26	66	92	107

Career Highlights

JOINED THE OSHAWA GENERALS JUNIOR A HOCKEY TEAM (1962–63) AT AGE 14

IN HIS ROOKIE JUNIOR SEASON, COMMUTED 300 MILES (ROUND TRIP) FROM HIS HOMETOWN OF PARRY SOUND FOR EACH GAME

WON THE CALDER TROPHY AS NHL'S TOP ROOKIE (1966–67)

WON THE NORRIS TROPHY AS THE LEAGUE'S TOP DEFENCEMAN THE NEXT EIGHT CONSECUTIVE SEASONS

VOTED TO THE NHL'S FIRST ALL-STAR TEAM EIGHT TIMES, SECOND ALL-STAR TEAM ONCE

TWICE LED BRUINS TO STANLEY CUP, IN 1969–70 AND 1971–72

FIRST DEFENCEMAN TO WIN NHL SCORING CROWN, IN 1969–70 AND AGAIN IN 1974–75

FIRST NHL PLAYER TO WIN THE LEAGUE'S MVP AWARD, THE HART TROPHY, IN THREE CONSECUTIVE SEASONS (1969–70 TO 1971–72)

TWICE VOTED CONN SMYTHE TROPHY WINNER (1969–70 AND 1971–72) AS OUTSTANDING PLAYER IN THE PLAYOFFS

SCORED 270 GOALS AND 645 ASSISTS IN 657 NHL REGULAR SEASON GAMES

SCORED 26 GOALS AND 66 ASSISTS IN 74 PLAYOFF GAMES

WON LOU MARSH TROPHY IN 1970 AS CANADA'S OUTSTANDING MALE ATHLETE

VOTED MVP OF THE 1976 CANADA CUP TOURNAMENT

HAD SIX CONSECUTIVE 100-POINT-PLUS SEASONS IN THE NHL FROM 1969–70 TO 1974–75

FAMOUS NO. 4 JERSEY RETIRED AT BOSTON GARDEN CEREMONY IN 1979

Acknowledgments

Grateful acknowledgment is made for permission to reprint the following newspaper article in this book:

Rimstead, Paul. "Bobby Orr – future superstar? Boston prospect well on his way." *Toronto Star*, January 11, 1964.

The editor wishes to express gratitude to Oshawa resident Babe Brown for her kind help in furnishing research material and opening up her personal collection of photographs and junior hockey memorabilia from Bobby Orr's Oshawa career.

The editor also wishes to thank Frank Orr, Jack Thompson, and William Kurelo for providing clippings, photos, mementos, and other hockey-related items that were invaluable in planning the scope of this book.

The editor also extends gratitude to Bob Hutton and Howard Elliott, who provided a Bobby Orr photograph from the Hamilton Spectator sports archives.

Grateful acknowledgement is made for use of photographs to the following: Hockey Hall of Fame (photos on jacket and pages ii, vi–vii, viii, 3, 4, 7, 8–9, 12, 20, 25, 26, 32, 34, 35, 36–37, 39, 40 (both), 44, 49, 52–53, 56, 57, 59, 60–61, 62, 64–65, 67 (both), 68, 71, 73, 76, 80, 83, 84–85, 86, 89, 92, 95, 96, 99, 100, 102, 104–5, 106 (all)); Babe Brown (photos on pages 14, 19, 28, 47); *Hamilton Spectator* sports archives (photo on page 16); Jack Thompson (both photos on page 79); Bill Douglas (photo on page 90).

Every effort has been made to secure permissions to reprint material reproduced in this book. The editor and publisher will gladly receive information that will enable them to rectify in subsequent editions of this book any inadvertent errors or omissions.

Also Available

Remembering the Rocket

A CELEBRATION

Craig MacInnis, Editor

Maurice "The Rocket" Richard has been called the greatest goal scorer in professional hockey history, not least for his astonishing feat of notching 50 goals in 50 games. Yet that alone hardly explains his legend.

Richard not only ushered in hockey's modern era with his prolific scoring touch and fiery play, he also came to symbolize the hopes and fears of an entire culture.

In the 1940s and '50s, Quebec wanted a hero and they found one in Richard – a fierce competitor, a skilful artist, and a proud warrior, whose famous temper triggered one of the darkest events in Canadian sporting history – the Montreal riot of 1955.

This look back at the greatest player to ever don the red, white, and blue includes some of the finest sportswriting of the era, documenting Richard the hero and Richard the villain, Richard the doting family man and Richard the aging hockey legend.

Passionate about everything in life, Richard raised the stakes for all of us who understand that hockey has always been more than just a game.

0-7737-31288 $26.95 CDN $19.95 US

Published by
Stoddart Publishing Co. Limited
34 Lesmill Road, Toronto, Canada M3B 2T6

For more information about this and other Stoddart books, visit our website
www.genpub.com/stoddart/books.html